YOUR KNOWLEDGE HAS VALUE

AF150741

- We will publish your bachelor's and master's thesis, essays and papers

- Your own eBook and book - sold worldwide in all relevant shops

- Earn money with each sale

Upload your text at www.GRIN.com
and publish for free

Jagrut Solanki

A Reinforcement Learning Network based Novel Adaptive Routing Algorithm for Wireless Ad-Hoc Network

GRIN Publishing

Bibliographic information published by the German National Library:

The German National Library lists this publication in the National Bibliography; detailed bibliographic data are available on the Internet at http://dnb.dnb.de .

Imprint:

Copyright © 2014 GRIN Verlag GmbH
Print and binding: Books on Demand GmbH, Norderstedt Germany
ISBN: 978-3-656-86327-4

This book at GRIN:

http://www.grin.com/en/e-book/286150/a-reinforcement-learning-network-based-novel-adaptive-routing-algorithm

GRIN - Your knowledge has value

Since its foundation in 1998, GRIN has specialized in publishing academic texts by students, college teachers and other academics as e-book and printed book. The website www.grin.com is an ideal platform for presenting term papers, final papers, scientific essays, dissertations and specialist books.

Visit us on the internet:

http://www.grin.com/

http://www.facebook.com/grincom

http://www.twitter.com/grin_com

A Reinforcement Learning Network based Novel Adaptive Routing Algorithm for Wireless Ad-Hoc Network

Abstract

A Wireless network is a collection of autonomous mobile nodes that communicate with each other over wireless links without any fixed infrastructure. It is a method by which homes, telecommunications networks and enterprise installations avoid the costly process of introducing cables into a building, or as a connection between various equipment locations. A routing protocol is taking a vital role in the modern Wireless Network. Mobile ad hoc network (MANET) is an autonomous system of mobile nodes connected by wireless links. Each node operates not only as an end system, but also as a router to forward packets .the nodes are free to move about and a network.a routing protocol which is responsible to determine how nodes communicate with each other and forward the packets through the optimal path to travel from a source node to a destination node. The purpose of paper is to contribute the study and comparison of routing protocols performance in MANET

Keywords: Wireless, Routing Protocol, AODV, DSR, ZRP..

Introduction

In the computing industry the importance of Wireless network is become very high. Wireless network are adapted to enable mobility to a great extend. There are two types of network they are Infra-structured network and ad-hoc network. In Infra-structured network have the network with fixed and wired gateway. In ad hoc networks, where all devices have equal status on a network and are free to associate with any other ad hoc network devices in link range. A mobile ad-hoc network is self-configuring network of mobile nodes which do not need any pre-existing infrastructure. In MANET the mobility of the nodes affects the performance of network. The network topology changes frequently due to mobility of nodes. In MANET each router has priori knowledge only of networks attached to it directly [1]. MANET is very attractive in tactical and military applications because of rapidly deployable and self-organizing configurability. Like tactical communications in a battlefield, where the environment is unfavorable, but fast network establishment self reconfiguration and security-sensitive operations are absolutely essential.

Data packets that successfully delivered to destinations that counted. It can be calculated as follows: Σ (arrive time – send time) / Σ Number of connections

OVERVIEW OF VARIOUS ON-DEMAND ROUTING PROTOCOLS

A routing protocol is the protocols that specify how routers communicate with each other, [2] disseminating information that enables them to select routes between any two nodes on a computer network

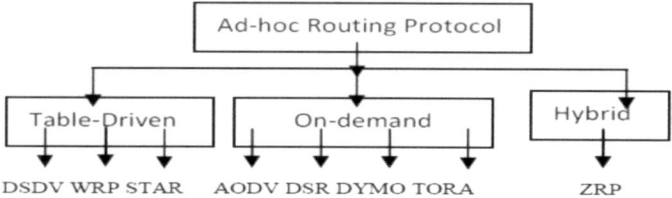

Figure 1: Categorization of Routing Protocols

Table Driven (proactive) Routing Protocol

The proactive routing protocol maintains its table in order to store routing information. Change in the network topology caused by anything need to be reflected to this table and propagate the updating information throughout the network [3].

DSDV

Destination Sequenced Distance Vector (DSDV) is a proactive routing protocol. Each mobile node maintains a routing table in which all the possible destinations and the number of hops to them in the network are stored. The entries in the table are updated periodically. It assigns sequence number to routing entries. During communication route with highest sequence number is selected, in case of same sequence number higher metric value route is selected [3].

On-Demand (Reactive) Routing Protocol

On Demand-Driven Protocol routes only when desired by source node. When a node requires a route to a destination, it initiates a route discovery process within the network [2] [3].On demand routing protocols were designed with the aim of reducing control overhead, thus increasing bandwidth and conserving power at the mobile stations

In On-Demand routing protocols, the routes are created as and when it is needed. Once a route has been established in the network, it is maintained until either the destination becomes inaccessible or until the route is no longer used [1].

Existing on-demand re-active routing protocols are:

A. DSR (Dynamic Source Routing),

B. AODV (ad hoc On-Demand Distance Vector Routing)

C. AOMDV (Ad-Hoc On-Demand Multi-Path Distance Vector Routing)

D. LAR (Location Aided Routing)

E. TORA (Temporally-Ordered Routing Algorithm)

F. ABR (Associatively Based Routing)

G. LMR (Light-Weight Mobile Routing)

H. SSA (Signal Stability Based Adaptive Routing Algorithm)

I. CBRP (Cluster Based Routing)

J. RDMAR (Relative Distance Micro-Discovery Ad-Hoc Routing)

K. MSR (Multi-Path Source Routing)

L. ARA (Ant-Colony Based Routing Algorithm)

AODV

AODV stands for Ad Hoc on Demand Distance Vector Protocol. AODV is a reactive Protocol, So the routes are created and maintained only when they are needed. The routing table stores the information about the next hop to the destination and a sequence number which is received from the destination and indicating the freshness of the received information. It also stores the information about the active neighbors is received throughout the discovery of the destination host. When the corresponding route breaks then the neighbors can be notified [2]. The source broadcasts a route request (RREQ) packet when it wants to find path to the destination. The neighbors in turn broadcast the packet to their neighbors until it reaches an intermediate node that has recent route information about the destination or until it reaches the destination. An already received route request packet is discarded by the nodes [4]. In AODV, whenever a source needs a path to the destination, it starts the route discovery by flooding the route request (RREQ) to the destination in the network and then waits for the route reply (RREP). If the intermediate node, which receives the first copy of RREQ, knows the destination node, it may unicast a route reply (RREP) back to the source node via the reverse path; otherwise, it re-broadcasts the RREQ packet. If the source receives the RREP, the forward path to the destination would be established. When a node discovers a link break, the node proceeds the local repair if the destination is nearby. If the destination is far away it broadcasts the RERR packet. The source, received the RERR message, tries to search the route to the destination again if the path is still needed[3]. AODV only supports one route for each destination. This causes a node to reinitiate a route request query when it's only route breaks. But if mobility increases route requests also increases [4].

DSR

Dynamic Source Routing (DSR) is an entirely on-demand ad hoc network routing protocol composed of two parts: Route Discovery and Route Maintenance [4]. DSR designed specifically for use in multi-hop wireless ad hoc networks of mobile nodes. DSR can interoperate with Mobile IP, and nodes using Mobile IP and DSR have seamlessly migrated between WLANs, cellular data services, and DSR mobile ad hoc networks [2]. DSR uses source routing, i.e. the source determines the complete sequence of hops that each packet should traverse. This requires that the sequence of hops is included in each packet's header.[6]. Finding a route is generally a costly operation in terms of time, bandwidth and energy. Advantage of source routing is that it avoids the need for up-to-date routing information in the intermediate is included in the packets. Finally, it avoids routing loops easily because the complete route is determined by a single node instead of making the decision hop-by-hop.

Hybrid Routing Protocols

Based on combination of both table and demand driven Routing protocols, some hybrid routing protocols are proposed to combine advantage of both proactive and reactive protocols. The most typical hybrid one is zone routing protocol.

ZRP

ZRP defines a zone whose radius is measured in terms of hops. Each node utilizes proactive routing within its zone and reactive routing outside of its zone. Hence, a given node knows the identity of and a route to all nodes within its zone. When the node has data packets for a particular destination, then it checks its routing table for a route. If the destination lies within the zone, a route will exist in the route table. Otherwise, if the destination is not within the zone, a search to find a route to that destination is needed [3]. It utilizes Interzone Routing Protocol (IERP) for discovering routes to destinations outside the zone.

COMPARISON OF ROUTING PROTOCOLS

Based on literature survey the comparison of routing protocols is as shown in the table below. The table below shows the basic category of protocol as well as the nature of routing. The table also specifies the advantages & disadvantages of them.

Methods	Proactive/ Reactive	Location Based/ Identity Based	Advantages	Disadvantages
AODV	Reactive	Identity Based	Loop free. Obtains routes Quickly. Decreases Routing overhead	Route discovery latency can be high for large network. Performs better only in low traffic
DSDV	Proactive	Identity Based	Loop Free Fast reaction to topology change	higher overhead as maintains routing information even when not Used.
DSR	Reactive	Identity Based	Lowest overhead as it Uses caching. Loop free routing. Lesser Packet loss	Higher delay in increased node speed
ZRP	Hybrid	Identity Based	Performs better for small size network	For large routing zone behaves like pure proactive & for small zone like Reactive. If network is large average Throughput decreases.

CONCLUSION

After performing survey and analyzing the protocols AODV, DSDV, DSR & ZRP on the basis of parameters overhead & packet delivery fraction, it is found that AODV protocol gives the better performance than the others. The performance depends on some factors like node speed, mobility and other scenarios.

REFERENCES

[1] Priyanka Makwana, D. G. (2014). "Cross Layer Approach For Routing Protocol and. International Journal of Enhanced Research in Management & Computer Applications" , 3 (2).

[2] Richa Sharma, R. M. (2014, January)." A Survey on Performance Analysis of AODV and DSR". IJESRT .

[3] UDAYSINGH A. BAGADE, S. S. (2014). "SURVEY OF ROUTING PROTOCOLS IN MANET". IJPRET , 2.

[4] Shaily Mittal, P. K. (2009)." PERFORMANCE COMPARISION OF AODV, DSR and ZRP ROUTING PROTOCOLS IN MANET'S". IEEE .

[5] Ashutosh Lanjewar, N. G. (2013)." Optimizing Cost, Delay, Packet Loss and Network Load in AODV Routing Protocol". IJCSIS , 11.

[6] Jonish Kumar, P. K. (2014, February 1). "Simulation Based Analysis of DSR, LAR and DREAM Routing Protocol for Mobile Ad hoc Networks." ICARI .